Measuring

Written by Peter Patilla

Illustrations by Liz Pichon

OXFORD
UNIVERSITY PRESS

OXFORD

UNIVERSITY PRESS

Great Clarendon Street, Oxford OX2 6DP

Oxford University Press is a department of the University of Oxford.
It furthers the University's objective of excellence in research, scholarship,
and education by publishing worldwide in

Oxford New York

Athens Auckland Bangkok Bogotá Buenos Aires Kolkata
Cape Town Chennai Dar es Salaam Delhi Florence Hong Kong Istanbul
Karachi Kuala Lumpur Madrid Melbourne Mexico City Mumbai
Nairobi Paris São Paulo Shanghai Singapore Taipei Tokyo Toronto Warsaw

with associated companies in Berlin Ibadan

Oxford is a registered trade mark of Oxford University Press
in the UK and in certain other countries

British Library Cataloguing in Publication Data available

H/b ISBN 0–19–910793–9
P/b ISBN 0–19–910794–7

1 3 5 7 9 10 8 6 4 2

Designed and Typeset by Perry Tate Design
Printed in Hong Kong

My name is

· ·

Notes for parents and teachers

This book develops early concepts of *measuring* for adults and children to enjoy and share together. It has been carefully written to introduce the key words and ideas related to *measuring* which children will meet in their first couple of years in school.

Throughout the book you will see **Word Banks** which contain the new mathematical words introduced for each concept. All the words from the word bank are gathered together at the back of the book. You can use the word banks with your child in several ways:

- See which of the words are recognized through games such as *I spy. I spy the word long – can you find it? I spy a word beginning with h – where is it?*
- Choose a word and ask your child to find it in the book.
- Let your child choose a word from the word bank at the back of the book, and say something about it.

Look for other opportunities in everyday life to use the ideas and vocabulary introduced in this book. Ask questions such as: Who has the largest piece? Whose glass is half full? Let your child order everyday things according to their size, asking Which is the longest? Which is the shortest? Bake a cake together to introduce practical measuring. Ensure that children realize that *measuring* is easy, and most importantly, fun.

Long and short

We measure things in different ways.

a long caterpillar

a short caterpillar

getting longer

getting shorter

longest

shortest

Which caterpillars are longer than this one? Which are shorter?

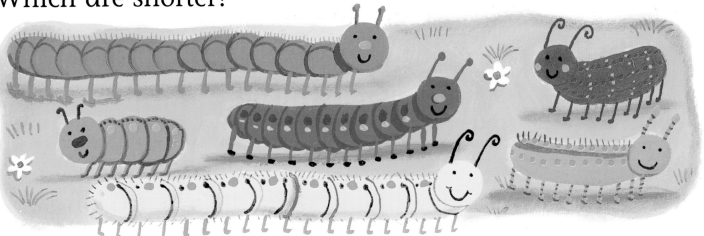

Which is the longest caterpillar?
Which is the shortest?

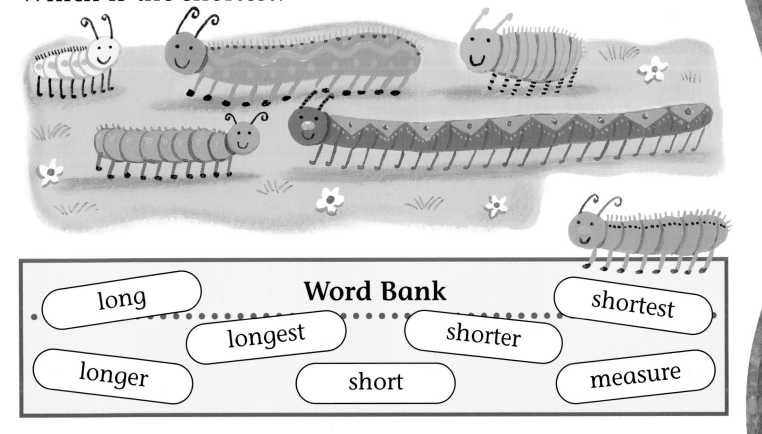

Word Bank

long

longest

shorter

shortest

longer

short

measure

5

Tall and short

There are tall and short things around us everywhere.

a tall flower

a short flower

getting taller

getting shorter

tallest

shortest

Which flowers are taller than this one?
Which are shorter?

Which is the tallest box?
Which is the shortest?

Word Bank

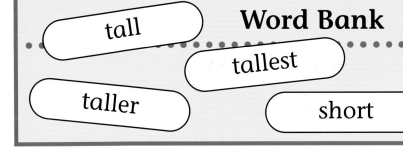

tall

tallest

taller

short

shorter

shortest

Opposites

Opposites are very different.

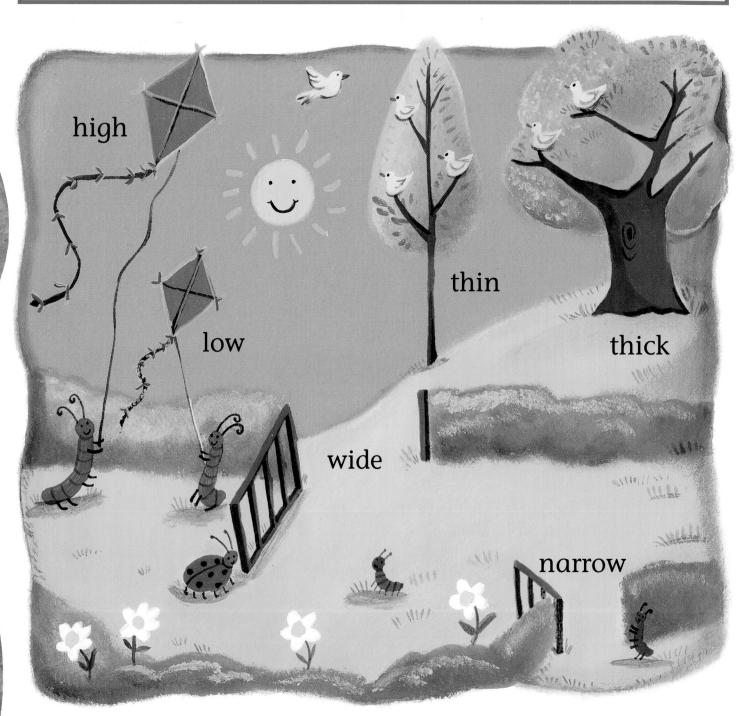

high

low

thin

thick

wide

narrow

8

Which bird is highest?
Which bird is lowest?

Which smile is widest?

Which sandwich is thickest?
Which is thinnest?

Word Bank

- high
- low
- wide
- narrow
- thick
- thin
- thickest
- thinnest
- highest
- lowest
- widest

Sizes

We use words such as large and small to measure size.

a large plant

a small plant

Some things are large.
Some things are small.

getting larger

getting smaller

Which is the smallest bottle?
Which is the largest tub?
Match the tops to their bottoms.

Word Bank

size   smaller

larger   small

large   largest   smallest

Distances

Distance is how far apart two things are.

far apart

close together

When talking about distances and sizes you can use words like length, width and height.

finding the length

finding the width

finding the height

Which word would you use to talk about these distances?

● length   ● width   ● height?

Who is furthest away from the tree?
Who is nearest?

Word Bank

(length)

(width)

(height)

(distance)

(close)

(far)

(furthest)

(nearest)

Centimetres and metres

We can use rulers to measure distances.

You measure short lengths and distances in centimetres.
Long lengths are measured in metres.
A metre is as long as one hundred centimetres.

This bean measures 11 cm.

The distance between the carrots is 8 cm.

A short way of writing centimetre is **cm**.
A short way of writing metre is **m**.

You use a ruler to measure short distances and lengths.
How long are each of these things?

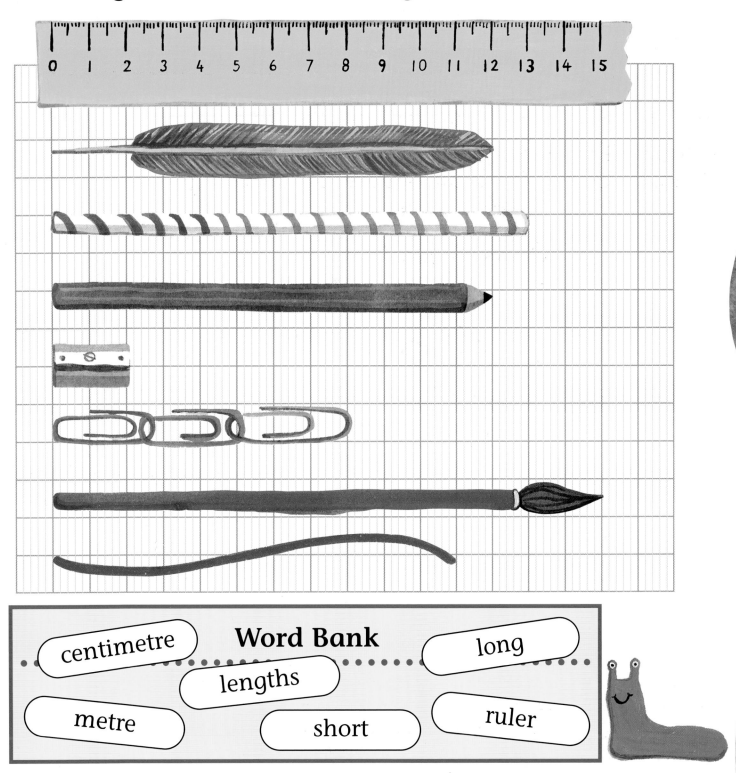

Word Bank

centimetre

lengths

long

metre

short

ruler

Heavy and light

Holding things can tell you whether they are heavier, lighter or about the same.

heavier   lighter

about the same

Sometimes you need a balance to find out which is heavier or which is lighter.

heavier   lighter   about the same

Which of these things do you think will be heavy?
Which will be light?

Which will be heaviest? Which will be lightest?
Which will be about the same weight?

Word Bank

heavy   light

heavier   lighter

heaviest   lightest

weight

same   balance

Grams and kilograms

You can find out how heavy something is by using a balance and weights.

Each weight has a number of grams or kilograms written on it.
A kilogram is as heavy as one thousand grams.

You can also use scales to find out how heavy things are.
The dial tells you how heavy the thing is.

A short way of writing gram is **g**.
A short way of writing kilogram is **kg**.

Light things are weighed in grams.
Heavy things are weighed in kilograms.

Look at these groups. Would the weight of each group
be weighed in grams or kilograms?

Word Bank

heavy   grams

weights   scales

light   balance   kilograms

Full and empty

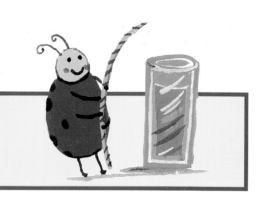

Things can be full, empty or in between.

full   nearly full   half full   nearly empty   empty

Sometimes we like things to be full.

Sometimes we like them to be empty.

Capacity is how much something holds.
A large capacity holds a lot.

A small capacity does not hold very much.

Which container do you think has the largest capacity?
Which has the smallest capacity?
Which container is about half full?
Which container is nearly empty?

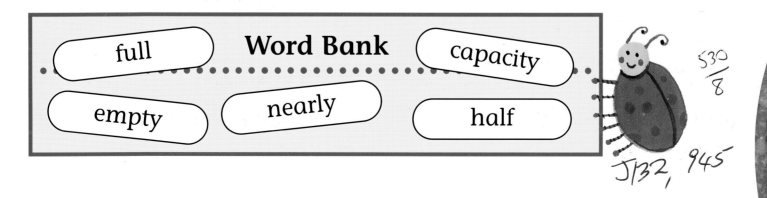

Word Bank

full   capacity

empty   nearly   half

Millilitres and litres

You can find the capacity of a liquid using a measuring jug.

A measuring jug has millilitres or litres written on it.
A litre is the same as one thousand millilitres.

The shape of a container can make a litre look very different.

A short way of writing litre is **l**.
A short way of writing millilitre is **ml**.

Which of these containers do you think holds more than a litre? Which holds less than a litre?

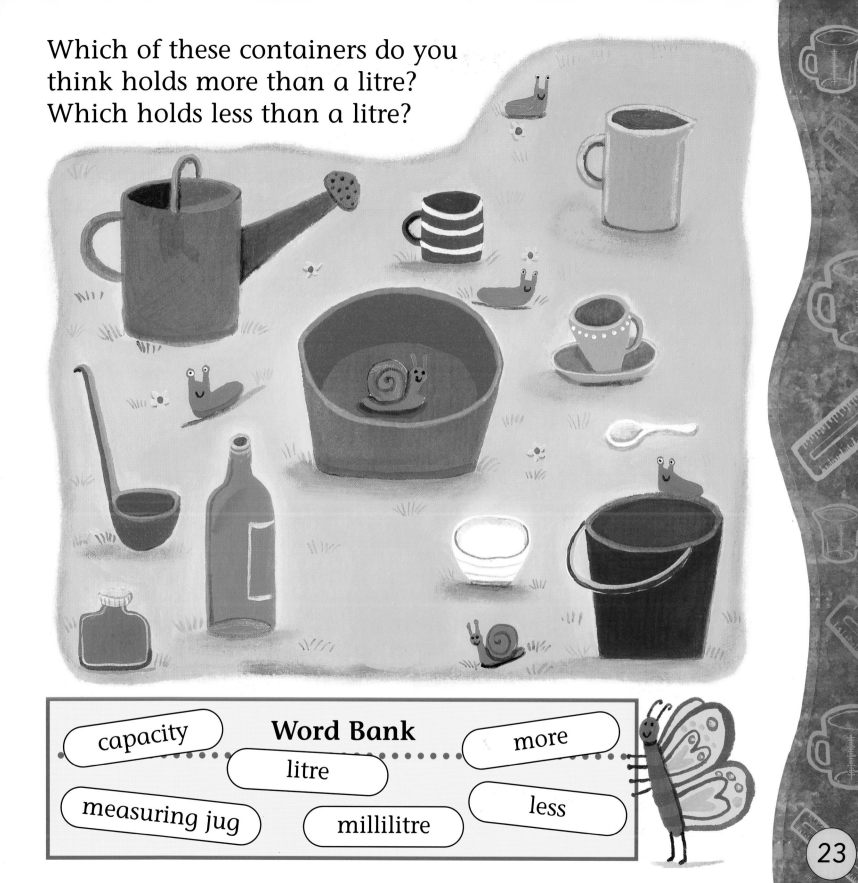

Word Bank

capacity
litre
more
measuring jug
millilitre
less

Temperature

Temperature is about whether things are cold, warm or hot.

cold

colder

coldest

hot

hotter

hottest

Thermometers are used to measure temperature.
They measure temperature in degrees.

Which of these are very hot?
Which are cold?
Which are boiling?
Which are freezing?

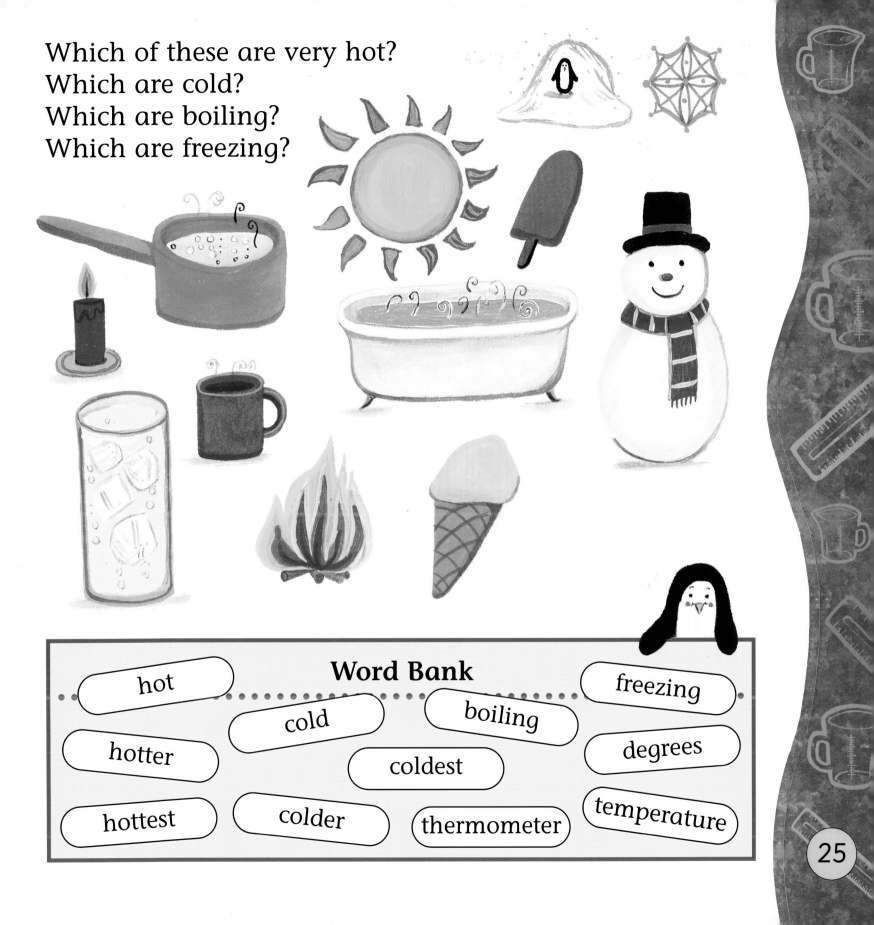

Word Bank

hot

cold

boiling

freezing

hotter

coldest

degrees

hottest

colder

thermometer

temperature

Measuring long ago

People have found different ways to measure.

Many years ago people used parts of their body to help them measure.

Cubit

A cubit is from finger tip to elbow.

Foot

All over the world the length of a foot was used.

Pace

Romans measured distances in paces. A thousand paces was called a mile.

Span

A span is the distance from the little finger to the thumb.

People have used all sorts of weights and balances.

Weights

Balances

Long ago weights used to be interesting shapes such as animals.

Simple balances have been around a long, long time.

Capacity has been measured with all sorts of containers.

Shells

Containers

All sorts of shells were used for measuring.

People started to measure using containers which were the same size.

Word Bank

Word Bank

Word Bank

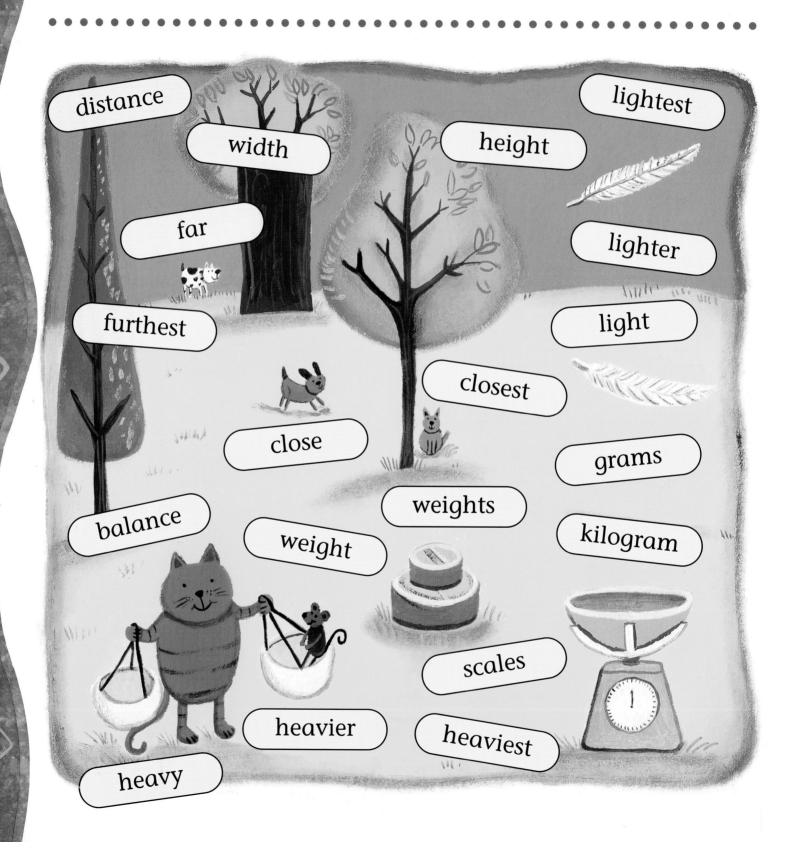

distance

lightest

width

height

far

lighter

furthest

light

closest

close

grams

weights

balance

weight

kilogram

scales

heavier

heaviest

heavy

Word Bank

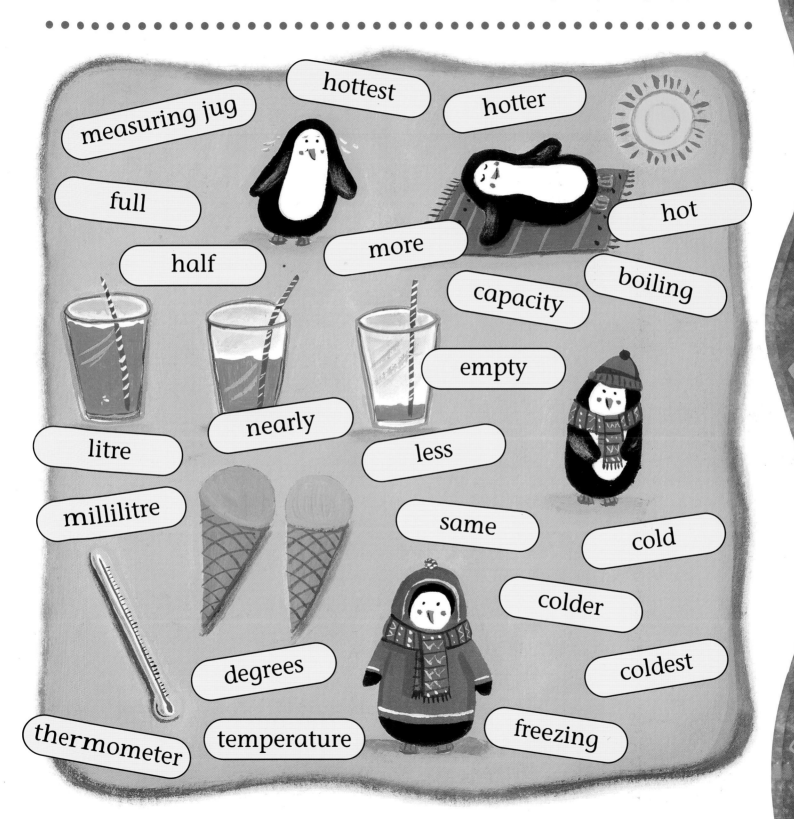

measuring jug

hottest

hotter

full

hot

half

more

boiling

capacity

empty

nearly

less

litre

millilitre

same

cold

colder

coldest

degrees

thermometer

temperature

freezing

Measuring quiz

Which is the tallest giraffe?
Which is the largest pig?
Who is eating something cold?
Who is drinking something hot?
Where is the smallest animal?
Who has their mouth open the widest?